CW01508735

A
Tradition
of
Prayer

CONTENTS

V. ANGELS AND SAINTS

VI. TIMES AND OCCASIONS

VII. INVOCATIONS

INTRODUCTION

It is through the liturgy that the Church best expresses its nature as the body of Christ. The Second Vatican Council began its work for renewal in the Church by renewing the liturgical forms and by promoting good celebration of public worship. At the same time, the Council encouraged personal prayer and devotion which are in harmony with the renewing liturgy.[1]

The liturgy is the public worship and prayer offered by Christ and his Church to the heavenly Father. This worship is our celebration of praise and thanks to God for having saved us through the death and resurrection of Jesus, his Son and our brother. The liturgy is also a way for God's people to exercise their priestly power with Jesus by offering sacrifice and interceding for the world.

The Second Vatican Council saw the liturgy as the source and summit of our Christian living. The liturgy is the source from which our daily life and our prayer derive their strength and power, and it is the goal toward which we direct all our actions. It is in our public worship, and especially in the eucharist, that we find the center of our life.

Personal prayer. Under the guidance of the Spirit, our personal prayer should be based on and flow from the Scriptures, the liturgy, the life of the Church, and our response to God's invitation. Our

---

[1] Vatican Council 11, Constitution on the Liturgy *Sacrosanctum Concilium*, 4 December 1963, art. 13:

"Popular devotions of the Christian people are to be highly endorsed, provided they accord with the laws and norms of the Church, above all when they are ordered by the Apostolic See.

"Devotions proper to particular Churches also have a special dignity if they are undertaken by mandate of the bishops according to customs or books lawfully approved.

"But these devotions should be so fashioned that they harmonize with the liturgical season, accord with the sacred liturgy, are in some way derived from it, and lead the people to it, since, in fact, the liturgy by its very nature far surpasses any of them." [Cited in *Documents on the Liturgy, 1963–1979. Conciliar, Papal, and Curial Texts*, trans. International Commission on English in the Liturgy (Collegeville, Minnesota, The Liturgical Press, 1982), document no. 1.]

prayer should bring us into closer union with Jesus and with his community, and lead us to a deeper sharing in the life and prayer of the people of God.

Guidelines for personal prayer. In 1974, Pope Paul VI offered several guidelines or criteria for devotion to Mary.[2] These may also serve as helpful guidelines for balanced personal and family prayer:

– *Biblical.* The Scriptures are inspired by the same Spirit who dwells in each Christian. The word of God is living and stands as the light for our paths. From the word we receive guidance, strength, consolation, correction. The Scriptures record God's love for us, his sending of his Son, the love of Jesus our Lord; they also invite us to respond by prayer in the words of Scripture, especially the psalms, and in our own words and actions as well.

– *Liturgical.* The liturgy serves as a good model for our family and personal prayer. In the liturgy we praise God for his greatness and thank him for his goodness to us. We pray to the Father, through and with Jesus his Son, in the Holy Spirit. We pray for the needs of all the world. The liturgy is the prayer of all God's people and is offered in union with the Church in heaven and on earth.

– *Ecumenical.* If we are faithful to our Lord's plea for unity among his followers (John 17), we need to be aware of the way our choice of popular prayers and devotions may affect other Christians. All exaggerations, legends, sheer sentimentality, and incorrect practices must be avoided, even when they are long-standing.[3]

– *Other criteria* for personal prayer and devotion are to be found in the way they help us to come closer to the Trinity, to Jesus Christ, and to his Church.[4]

These guidelines will help us to assess the value and usefulness of the prayers and devotions in this book, for it is in light of these guidelines that the International Commission on English in the

[2] See Apostolic Exhortation Marialis Cultus of His Holiness Paul VI: On the Proper Forms of Marian Devotion and on Its Increase (2 February 1974): nos. 29-33, in Documents on the Liturgy, no. 467.

[3] *Ibid.,* nos. 38 and 31.

[4] *Ibid.,* nos. 25–27.

Liturgy (ICEL) has undertaken this work of providing a contemporary translation of these prayers.

* * *

In 1968, a collection of some of the prayers used by Catholics through the centuries was published in Latin by the Holy See.[5]

To foster further prayer among the faithful, some bishops have requested that the prayers in this document be translated by ICEL in a language and style suitable to the needs of the contemporary Church. It was judged that such a translation was needed for several reasons:

– No uniform translation is available for English-speaking countries.

– Existing translations sometimes need revision in order to express sound contemporary theology and spirituality. Since many of these prayers, however, have been memorized by Catholics, revisions have been weighed with great care.

– A modified translation of these texts, with words and expressions congenial to our times, will encourage their use among new generations of Catholics.

---

[5] In this publication, *Enchiridion Indulgentiarum; Normae et Concessiones*, 1968, the Holy See included a document on the nature of indulgences. A translation of this document is included in ICEL's *Documents on the Liturgy*, no. 390.

Nihil obstat   Father Anton Cowan *Censor*
Imprimatur   Rt. Rev. Vincent Nichols, V.G.
Westminster   15th August 1999

The Nihil obstat *and* Imprimatur *are a declaration that a book or pamphlet is considered to be free from doctrinal or moral error. It is not implied that those who have granted the* Nihil obstat *and* Imprimatur *agree with the contents, opinions or statements expressed.*

I
MASS AND
HOLY COMMUNION

1 PRAYER OF SAINT AMBROSE

Lord Jesus Christ
I approach your banquet table
in fear and trembling,
for I am a sinner
and dare not rely on my own worth
but only on your goodness and mercy.
I am defiled by many sins in body and soul
and by my unguarded thoughts and words.

Gracious God of majesty and awe,
I seek your protection,
I look for your healing.
Poor troubled sinner that I am,
I appeal to you, the fountain of all mercy.
I cannot bear your judgment,
but I trust in your salvation.
Lord, I show my wounds to you
and uncover my shame before you.
I know my sins are many and great,
and they fill me with fear,
but I hope in your mercies,
for they cannot be numbered.

Lord Jesus Christ, eternal king,
divine and human,
crucified for humanity,
look upon me with mercy and hear my prayer,
for I trust in you.
Have mercy on me,
full of sorrow and sin,
for the depth of your compassion never ends.
Praise to you, saving sacrifice,
offered on the wood of the cross for me and for all.
Praise to the noble and precious blood,
flowing from the wounds of my crucified Lord Jesus Christ
and washing away the sins of the whole world.

Remember, Lord, your creature,
whom you have redeemed with your blood.
I repent of my sins,
and I long to put right what I have done.

Merciful Father, take away all my offenses and sins;
purify me in body and soul,
and make me worthy to taste the holy of holies.
May your body and blood,
which I intend to receive, although I am unworthy,
be for me the remission of my sins,
the washing away of my guilt,
the end of my evil thoughts,
and the rebirth of my better instincts.
May it spur me on to works pleasing to you
and be profitable to my health in body and soul
and a firm defense against the wiles of my enemies.
Amen.

– Attributed to St. Ambrose, c. 339–397, bishop of Milan.

Almighty and ever-living God,
I approach the sacrament of your only-begotten Son,
    our Lord Jesus Christ.
I come sick to the doctor of life,
unclean to the fountain of mercy,
blind to the radiance of eternal light,
poor and needy to the Lord of heaven and earth.

Lord, in your great generosity,
heal my sickness, wash away my defilement,
enlighten my blindness, enrich my poverty,
and clothe my nakedness.

May I receive the bread of angels,
the King of kings and Lord of lords,
with humble reverence,
with the purity and faith,
the repentance and love,
and the determined purpose
that will help to bring me to salvation.
May I receive the sacrament of the Lord's body and blood,
and its reality and power.

Kind God,
may I receive the body of your only-begotten Son,
    our Lord Jesus Christ,
born from the womb of the Virgin Mary,
and so be received into his mystical body
and numbered among his members.

Loving Father,
as on my earthly pilgrimage
I now receive your beloved Son
under the veil of a sacrament,
may I one day see him face to face in glory,
who lives and reigns with you for ever.
Amen.

– Attributed to St. Thomas Aquinas, c. 1225–1274.

3 A PRIEST'S PRAYER

My purpose is to celebrate Mass
and to make present the body and blood of our Lord Jesus Christ
according to the rite of the holy Roman Church
to the praise of our all-powerful God
and all his assembly in the glory of heaven,
for my good and the good of the pilgrim Church on earth,
and for all who have asked me to pray for them
in general and in particular,
and for the good of the holy Roman Church.

May the almighty and merciful Lord
grant us joy and peace,
amendment of life,
room for true repentance,
the grace and comfort of the Holy Spirit,
and perseverance in good works.
Amen.

4. ANIMA CHRISTI

Soul of Christ, sanctify me.
Body of Christ, heal me.
Blood of Christ, drench me.
Water from the side of Christ, wash me.
Passion of Christ, strengthen me.

Good Jesus, hear me.

In your wounds shelter me.
From turning away keep me.
From the evil one protect me.
At the hour of my death call me.
Into your presence lead me,
to praise you with all your saints
for ever and ever.
Amen .

> *– Early fourteenth century, familiar in English*
> *as the hymn* Soul of my Savior.

5. PRAYER BEFORE A CRUCIFIX

Good and gentle Jesus,
I kneel before you.
I see and I ponder your five wounds.
My eyes behold what David prophesied about you:
"They have pierced my hands and feet;
they have counted all my bones."

Engrave on me this image of yourself.
Fulfill the yearnings of my heart:
give me faith, hope, and love,
repentance for my sins,
and true conversion of life.
Amen.

> *– From the thanksgiving after Mass as given in the*
> *Roman Missal since 1570.*

6 O SACRUM CONVIVIUM

How holy this feast
in which Christ is our food:
his passion is recalled,
grace fills our hearts,
and we receive a pledge of the glory to come.

V. You gave them bread from heaven to be their food.
R. And this bread contained all goodness.

Let us pray.

Lord Jesus Christ,
you gave us the eucharist
as the memorial of your suffering and death.
May our worship of this sacrament of your body and blood
help us to experience the salvation you won for us
and the peace of the kingdom
where you live with the Father and the Holy Spirit,
one God, for ever and ever.

R. Amen.

*Antiphon from Evening Prayer II of Corpus Christi, attributed
to St. Thomas Aquinas (c. 1225–1274); versicle and response
from Midday Prayer, Corpus Christi; the prayer from the Solemnity at
Corpus Christi in* The Roman Missal.

7 TANTUM ERGO

Secret past imagination, dazzling and compelling awe;
Sacrament and celebration richer than the ancient law:
Faith can see by revelation more than senses ever saw.

Praise the Lord with exultation for the marvels he has done:
Blessing, power, and adoration to the Father and the Son
For creation and salvation; and the Spirit, Three in One. Amen.

– Last two verses of the hymn Pange, lingua,
written about 1264 by St. Thomas Aquinas (c. 1225–1274)

8 ADORO TE

Hidden here before me, Lord, I worship you,
Hidden in these symbols, yet completely true.
Lord, my soul surrenders, longing to obey,
And in contemplation wholly faints away.

Seeing, touching, tasting: these are all deceived;
Only through the hearing can it be believed.
Nothing is more certain: Christ has told me so;
What the Truth has uttered, I believe and know.

Only God was hidden when you came to die:
Human nature also here escapes the eye.
Both are my profession, both are my belief:
Bring me to your Kingdom, like the dying thief.

I am not like Thomas, who could see and touch;
Though your wounds are hidden, I believe as much.
Let me say so boldly, meaning what I say,
Loving you and trusting, now and every day.

Record of the Passion when the Lamb was slain,
Living bread that brings us back to life again:
Feed me with your presence, make me live on you;
Let that lovely fragrance fill me through and through.

Once a nesting pelican gashed herself to blood
For the preservation of her starving brood:
Now heal me with your blood, take away my guilt:
All the world is ransomed if one drop is spilt.

Jesus, for the present seen as through a mask,
Give me what I thirst for, give me what I ask:
Let me see your glory in a blaze of light,
And instead of blindness give me, Lord, my sight. Amen.

– Attributed to St. Thomas Aquinas (c. 1225–1274).

9 PRAYER OF THANKSGIVING AFTER MASS

Lord, Father all-powerful and ever-living God,
I thank you,
for even though I am a sinner, and your unprofitable servant,
you have fed me
with the precious body and blood of your Son, our Lord
  Jesus Christ
not because of my worth but out of your kindness and your mercy.

I pray that this holy communion
may not bring me condemnation and punishment
but forgiveness and salvation.
May it be a helmet of faith and a shield of good will.
May it purify me from evil ways
and put an end to my evil passions.
May it bring me charity and patience,
humility and obedience,
and growth in the power to do good.
May it be my strong defense
against all my enemies, visible and invisible,
and the perfect calming of all my evil impulses,
bodily and spiritual.
May it unite me more closely to you,
the one true God,
and lead me safely through death
to everlasting happiness with you.

And I pray that you will lead me, a sinner,
to the banquet where you,
with your Son and the Holy Spirit,
are true and perfect light,
total fulfillment, everlasting joy,
gladness without end,
and perfect happiness to your saints.
Grant this through Christ our Lord.
Amen.

–Attributed to St. Thomas Aquinas (c. 1225–1274).

10 PRAYER OF SELF-DEDICATION TO JESUS CHRIST

Lord Jesus Christ,
take all my freedom,
my memory, my understanding, and my will.
All that I have and cherish
you have given me.
I surrender it all to be guided by your will.
Your grace and your love
are wealth enough for me.
Give me these, Lord Jesus,
and I ask for nothing more.

– Attributed to St. Ignatius Loyola (c. 1491–1556).

II
CREEDS AND CANTICLES

11 APOSTLES' CREED

I believe in God, the Father almighty,
 creator of heaven and earth.

I believe in Jesus Christ, his only Son, our Lord.
 He was conceived by the power of the Holy Spirit
  and born of the Virgin Mary.
 He suffered under Pontius Pilate,
  was crucified, died, and was buried.
 He descended to the dead.
 On the third day he rose again.
 He ascended into heaven,
  and is seated at the right hand of the Father.
 He will come again to judge the living and the dead.

I believe in the Holy Spirit,
 the holy catholic Church,
 the communion of saints,
 the forgiveness of sins,
 the resurrection of the body,
 and the life everlasting. Amen.

    – Based upon baptismal documents of the eighth century
      but related to texts of an earlier origin.

12 NICENE CREED

We believe in one God,
  the Father, the Almighty,
  maker of heaven and earth,
  of all that is, seen and unseen.

We believe in one Lord, Jesus Christ,
  the only Son of God,
  eternally begotten of the Father,
  God from God, Light from Light,
  true God from true God,
  begotten, not made,
  of one Being with the Father.
  Through him all things were made.
  For us men and for our salvation
    he came down from heaven:
  by the power of the Holy Spirit
    he became incarnate from the Virgin Mary, and was made man.
  For our sake he was crucified under Pontius Pilate;
    he suffered death and was buried.
    On the third day he rose again
      in accordance with the Scriptures;
    he ascended into heaven
      and is seated at the right hand of the Father.
  He will come again in glory to judge the living and the dead,
    and his kingdom will have no end.

We believe in the Holy Spirit, the Lord, the giver of life,
  who proceeds from the Father [and the Son].
  With the Father and the Son he is worshiped and glorified.
  He has spoken through the Prophets.
  We believe in one holy catholic and apostolic Church.
  We acknowledge one baptism for the forgiveness of sins.
  We look for the resurrection of the dead,
    and the life of the world to come. Amen.

– Drawn up, except for the Filioque,
by the Councils of Nicaea (325) and Constantinople (381).
It began to be used in the eucharistic liturgy
in the late fifth century in the East
and in the late sixth century in the West.

13 BENEDICTUS

Blessed be the Lord, the God of Israel;
he has come to his people and set them free.

He has raised up for us a mighty savior,
born of the house of his servant David.

Through his holy prophets he promised of old
    that he would save us from our enemies,
    from the hands of all who hate us.

He promised to show mercy to our fathers
and to remember his holy covenant.

This was the oath he swore to our father Abraham:
to set us free from the hands of our enemies,
free to worship him without fear,
holy and righteous in his sight
    all the days of our life.

You, my child, shall be called the prophet of the Most High,
for you will go before the Lord to prepare his way,
to give his people knowledge of salvation
by the forgiveness of their sins.

In the tender compassion of our God
the dawn from on high shall break upon us,
to shine on those who dwell in darkness and the shadow of death,
and to guide our feet into the way of peace.

– Luke 1:68–79.

―――◄

14 MAGNIFICAT

My soul proclaims the greatness of the Lord,
my spirit rejoices in God my Savior;
for he has looked with favor on his lowly servant.

From this day all generations will call me blessed:
the Almighty has done great things for me,
and holy is his Name.

17

He has mercy on those who fear him
in every generation.

He has shown the strength of his arm,
he has scattered the proud in their conceit.

He has cast down the mighty from their thrones,
and has lifted up the lowly.

He has filled the hungry with good things,
and the rich he has sent away empty.

He has come to the help of his servant Israel
for he has remembered his promise of mercy,
the promise he made to our fathers,
to Abraham and his children for ever.

– Luke 1:46–55.

———

15 NUNC DIMITTIS

Lord, now you let your servant go in peace;
your word has been fulfilled:

my own eyes have seen the salvation
which you have prepared in the sight of every people:

a light to reveal you to the nations
and the glory of your people Israel.

– Luke 2:29–32.

16 TE DEUM

You are God: we praise you;
You are the Lord: we acclaim you;
You are the eternal Father:
All creation worships you.

To you all angels, all the powers of heaven,
Cherubim and Seraphim, sing in endless praise:
    Holy, holy, holy Lord, God of power and might,
    heaven and earth are full of your glory.

The glorious company of apostles praise you.
The noble fellowship of prophets praise you.
The white-robed army of martyrs praise you.

Throughout the world the holy Church acclaims you:
    Father, of majesty unbounded,
your true and only Son, worthy of all worship,
    and the Holy Spirit, advocate and guide.

You, Christ, are the king of glory,
the eternal Son of the Father.

When you became man to set us free
you did not spurn the Virgin's womb.

You overcame the sting of death,
and opened the kingdom of heaven to all believers.

You are seated at God's right hand in glory.
We believe that you will come, and be our judge.

    Come then, Lord, and help your people,
    bought with the price of your own blood,
    and bring us with your saints
    to glory everlasting.

V. Save your people, Lord, and bless your inheritance.
R. Govern and uphold them now and always.
V. Day by day we bless you.

R. We praise your name for ever.
V. Keep us today, Lord, from all sin.
R. Have mercy on us, Lord, have mercy.
V. Lord, show us your love and mercy;
R. for we put our trust in you.
V. In you, Lord, is our hope:
R. and we shall never hope in vain.

– Fourth century, perhaps by St. Nicetas of Remesiana (335–415).

III
CONSECRATIONS AND LITANIES

17 ACT OF REPARATION TO THE SACRED HEART

Most loving Jesus,
how great is the love which you have poured out upon the world.
How casual and careless is our response!
Kneeling before you, we wish to atone
for the indifference and the slights which pierce you to the heart.

R. Praise to the heart of Jesus, our Savior and our God.

We ask forgiveness for our own shameful neglect.
We wish to make amends
for those who are obstinate in their unbelief,
for those who turn away from the light
and wander like sheep without a shepherd;
and for those who have broken their baptismal promises
and reject the gentle yoke of your law.

R. Praise to the heart of Jesus, our Savior and our God.

We wish to make amends for the sins of our society:
for lust and degradation,
for the corruption of the young,
for indifference and blasphemy,
for attacks against your Church,
for irreverence and even sacrilege
against your love in this blessed sacrament,
and for the public defiance of your law.

R. Praise to the heart of Jesus, our Savior and our God.

These are the sins for which you died,
but now we share in your atonement
by offering on the altar in union with you
the living sacrifice you made on the cross,
joining to it the sufferings of your Virgin Mother,
and those of all the saints and the whole Church.

R. Praise to the heart of Jesus, our Savior and our God.

We promise faithfully
that by your grace
we shall make reparation for our own sins
and for those of others
by a strong faith,
by holy living,
and by obedience to the law of the Gospel,
whose greatest commandment is that of charity.

R. Praise to the heart of Jesus, our Savior and our God.

We also promise to do our best
to discourage others from insulting you
and bring those we can to follow you.

R. Praise to the heart of Jesus, our Savior and our God.

Jesus, Lord,
receive this loving act of homage
together with the prayers of our Lady,
who stood by the cross,
our model in reparation.
Keep us faithful, even to the point of death,
give us the gift of perseverance
and lead us all to our promised land in heaven,
where you, with the Father and the Holy Spirit,
live and reign for ever and ever. Amen.

R. Praise to the heart of Jesus, our Savior and our God.

*— Prescribed by Pius XI (1857–1939) to be said on the feast
of the Sacred Heart. Although this prayer may be used privately,
it has been divided into sections with a refrain for public use.*

Loving Jesus, Redeemer of the world,
we are yours, and yours we wish to be.
To bind ourselves to you even more closely
we kneel before you today
and offer ourselves to your most Sacred Heart.

R. Praise to you, our Savior and our King.

Have mercy on all who have never known you
and on all who reject you and refuse to obey you:
gentle Lord, draw them to yourself.

R. Praise to you, our Savior and our King.

Reign over the faithful who have never left you,
reign over those who have squandered their inheritance,
the prodigal children who now are starving:
bring them back to their Father's house.

R. Praise to you, our Savior and our King.

Reign over those who are misled by error or divided by discord.
Hasten the day when we shall be one in faith and truth,
one flock with you, the one Shepherd.
Give to your Church freedom and peace,
and to all nations justice and order.
Make the earth resound from pole to pole with a single cry:
Praise to the Divine Heart that gained our salvation;
glory and honor be his for ever and ever. Amen.

R. Praise to you, our Savior and our King.

*—Originally written and prescribed by Leo XIII (1810–1903) for the
feast of the Sacred Heart. In 1925 Pius XI transferred it to
the new feast of Christ the King.*

Lord, have mercy	Lord, have mercy
Christ, have mercy	Christ, have mercy
Lord, have mercy	Lord, have mercy
God our Father in heaven	have mercy on us
God the Son, Redeemer of the world	have mercy on us
God the Holy Spirit	have mercy on us
Holy Trinity, one God	have mercy on us
Jesus, Son of the living God	have mercy on us
Jesus, splendor of the Father	have mercy on us
Jesus, brightness of everlasting light	have mercy on us
Jesus, king of glory	have mercy on us
Jesus, dawn of justice	have mercy on us
Jesus, Son of the Virgin Mary	have mercy on us
Jesus, worthy of our love	have mercy on us
Jesus, worthy of our wonder	have mercy on us
Jesus, mighty God	have mercy on us
Jesus, father of the world to come	have mercy on us
Jesus, prince of peace	have mercy on us
Jesus, all-powerful	have mercy on us
Jesus, pattern of patience	have mercy on us
Jesus, model of obedience	have mercy on us
Jesus, gentle and humble of heart	have mercy on us
Jesus, lover of chastity	have mercy on us
Jesus, lover of us all	have mercy on us
Jesus, God of peace	have mercy on us
Jesus, author of life	have mercy on us
Jesus, model of goodness	have mercy on us
Jesus, seeker of souls	have mercy on us
Jesus, our God	have mercy on us
Jesus, our refuge	have mercy on us
Jesus, father of the poor	have mercy on us
Jesus, treasure of the faithful	have mercy on us

Jesus, Good Shepherd — have mercy on us
Jesus, the true light — have mercy on us
Jesus, eternal wisdom — have mercy on us
Jesus, infinite goodness — have mercy on us

Jesus, our way and our life — have mercy on us
Jesus, joy of angels — have mercy on us
Jesus, king of patriarchs — have mercy on us
Jesus, teacher of apostles — have mercy on us
Jesus, master of evangelists — have mercy on us
Jesus, courage of martyrs — have mercy on us
Jesus, light of confessors — have mercy on us
Jesus, purity of virgins — have mercy on us
Jesus, crown of all saints — have mercy on us

Lord, be merciful — Jesus, save your people
From all evil — Jesus, save your people
From every sin — Jesus, save your people
From the snares of the devil — Jesus, save your people
From your anger — Jesus, save your people
From the spirit of infidelity — Jesus, save your people
From everlasting death — Jesus, save your people
From neglect of your Holy Spirit — Jesus, save your people

By the mystery of your incarnation — Jesus, save your people
By your birth — Jesus, save your people
By your childhood — Jesus, save your people
By your hidden life — Jesus, save your people
By your public ministry — Jesus, save your people
By your agony and crucifixion — Jesus, save your people
By your abandonment — Jesus, save your people
By your grief and sorrow — Jesus, save your people
By your death and burial — Jesus, save your people
By your rising to new life — Jesus, save your people
By your return in glory to the Father — Jesus, save your people
By your gift of the holy eucharist — Jesus, save your people
By your joy and glory — Jesus, save your people

Christ, hear us
Lord Jesus, hear our prayer

Christ, hear us
Lord Jesus, hear our prayer

Lamb of God, you take away
   the sins of the world

                have mercy on us

Lamb of God, you take away
   the sins of the world

                have mercy on us

Lamb of God, you take away
   the sins of the world

                have mercy on us

Let us pray.

Lord,
may we who honor the holy name of Jesus
enjoy his friendship in this life
and be filled with eternal joy in the kingdom
where he lives and reigns for ever and ever.

R. Amen.

> —*The origins of this litany, a commentary on Philippians 2:9–11, can be traced back to the fifteenth century, and some of the invocations, in a more elaborate form, are in the Litany of our Blessed Savior found in seventeenth century manuals. In its present form it was approved by Leo XIII (1810–1903) for use throughout the world.*

Lord, have mercy	Lord, have mercy
Christ, have mercy	Christ, have mercy
Lord, have mercy	Lord, have mercy
God our Father in heaven	have mercy on us
God the Son, Redeemer of the world	have mercy on us
God the Holy Spirit	have mercy on us
Holy Trinity, one God	have mercy on us
Heart of Jesus, Son of the eternal Father	have mercy on us
Heart of Jesus, formed by the Holy Spirit in the womb of the Virgin Mother	have mercy on us
Heart of Jesus, one with the eternal Word	have mercy on us
Heart of Jesus, infinite in majesty	have mercy on us
Heart of Jesus, holy temple of God	have mercy on us
Heart of Jesus, tabernacle of the Most High	have mercy on us
Heart of Jesus, house of God and gate of heaven	have mercy on us
Heart of Jesus, aflame with love for us	have mercy on us
Heart of Jesus, source of justice and love	have mercy on us
Heart of Jesus, full of goodness and love	have mercy on us
Heart of Jesus, well-spring of all virtue	have mercy on us
Heart of Jesus, worthy of all praise	have mercy on us
Heart of Jesus, king and center of all hearts	have mercy on us
Heart of Jesus, treasure-house of wisdom and knowledge	have mercy on us
Heart of Jesus, in whom there dwells the fullness of God	have mercy on us
Heart of Jesus, in whom the Father is well pleased	have mercy on us
Heart of Jesus, from whose fullness we have all received	have mercy on us
Heart of Jesus, desire of the eternal hills	have mercy on us
Heart of Jesus, patient and full of mercy	have mercy on us
Heart of Jesus, generous to all who turn to you	have mercy on us

Heart of Jesus, fountain of life and holiness	have mercy on us
Heart of Jesus, atonement for our sins	have mercy on us
Heart of Jesus, overwhelmed with insults	have mercy on us
Heart of Jesus, broken for our sins	have mercy on us
Heart of Jesus, obedient even to death	have mercy on us
Heart of Jesus, pierced by a lance	have mercy on us
Heart of Jesus, source of all consolation	have mercy on us
Heart of Jesus, our life and resurrection	have mercy on us
Heart of Jesus, our peace and reconciliation	have mercy on us
Heart of Jesus, victim for our sins	have mercy on us
Heart of Jesus, salvation of all who trust in you	have mercy on us
Heart of Jesus, hope of all who die in you	have mercy on us
Heart of Jesus, delight of all the saints	have mercy on us

Lamb of God, you take away the sins of the world	have mercy on us
Lamb of God, you take away the sins of the world	have mercy on us
Lamb of God, you take away the sins of the world	have mercy on us

V. Jesus, gentle and humble of heart.
R. Touch our hearts and make them like your own.

Let us pray.

Father,
we rejoice in the gifts of love
we have received from the heart of Jesus your Son.
Open our hearts to share his life
and continue to bless us with his love.
We ask this in the name of Jesus the Lord.

R. Amen.

—Many of the invocations in this litany can be traced to the seventeenth century. The litany was approved by Leo XIII (1810–1903).

21 LITANY OF THE PRECIOUS BLOOD

Lord, have mercy	Lord, have mercy
Christ, have mercy	Christ, have mercy
Lord, have mercy	Lord, have mercy

God our Father in heaven	have mercy on us
God the Son, Redeemer of the world	have mercy on us
God the Holy Spirit	have mercy on us
Holy Trinity, one God	have mercy on us

Blood of Christ, only Son of the Father	be our salvation
Blood of Christ, incarnate Word	be our salvation
Blood of Christ, of the new and eternal covenant	be our salvation
Blood of Christ, that spilled to the ground	be our salvation
Blood of Christ, that flowed at the scourging	be our salvation
Blood of Christ, dripping from the thorns	be our salvation
Blood of Christ, shed on the cross	be our salvation
Blood of Christ, the price of our redemption	be our salvation
Blood of Christ, our only claim to pardon	be our salvation
Blood of Christ, our blessing cup	be our salvation
Blood of Christ, in which we are washed	be our salvation
Blood of Christ, torrent of mercy	be our salvation
Blood of Christ, that overcomes evil	be our salvation
Blood of Christ, strength of the martyrs	be our salvation
Blood of Christ, endurance of the saints	be our salvation
Blood of Christ, that makes the barren fruitful	be our salvation
Blood of Christ, protection of the threatened	be our salvation
Blood of Christ, comfort of the weary	be our salvation
Blood of Christ, solace of the mourner	be our salvation
Blood of Christ, hope of the repentant	be our salvation
Blood of Christ, consolation of the dying	be our salvation
Blood of Christ, our peace and refreshment	be our salvation
Blood of Christ, our pledge of life	be our salvation
Blood of Christ, by which we pass to glory	be our salvation
Blood of Christ, most worthy of honor	be our salvation

Lamb of God, you take away
   the sins of the world   have mercy on us
Lamb of God, you take away
   the sins of the world   have mercy on us
Lamb of God, you take away
   the sins of the world   have mercy on us

V. Lord, you redeemed us by your blood.
R. You have made us a kingdom to serve our God.

Let us pray.

Father,
by the blood of your Son
you have set us free and saved us from death.
Continue your work of love within us,
that by constantly celebrating the mystery of our salvation
we may reach the eternal life it promises.
We ask this through Christ our Lord.

R. Amen

—This litany was approved by Pope John XXIII (1881–1963)
for the universal Church.

Lord, have mercy   Lord, have mercy
Christ, have mercy   Christ, have mercy
Lord, have mercy   Lord, have mercy

God our Father in heaven   have mercy on us
God the Son, Redeemer of the world   have mercy on us
God the Holy Spirit   have mercy on us
Holy Trinity, one God   have mercy on us

Holy Mary   pray for us
Holy Mother of God   pray for us
Most honored of virgins   pray for us

Mother of Christ   pray for us
Mother of the Church   pray for us
Mother of divine grace   pray for us
Mother most pure   pray for us
Mother of chaste love   pray for us
Mother and virgin   pray for us
Sinless Mother   pray for us
Dearest of mothers   pray for us
Model of motherhood   pray for us
Mother of good counsel   pray for us
Mother of our Creator   pray for us
Mother of our Savior   pray for us
Virgin most wise   pray for us
Virgin rightly praised   pray for us
Virgin rightly renowned   pray for us
Virgin most powerful   pray for us
Virgin gentle in mercy   pray for us
Faithful Virgin   pray for us
Mirror of justice   pray for us
Throne of wisdom   pray for us
Cause of our joy   pray for us

Shrine of the Spirit   pray for us
Glory of Israel   pray for us
Vessel of selfless devotion   pray for us
Mystical Rose   pray for us
Tower of David   pray for us

33

Tower of ivory	pray for us
House of gold	pray for us
Ark of the covenant	pray for us
Gate of heaven	pray for us
Morning Star	pray for us
Health of the sick	pray for us
Refuge of sinners	pray for us
Comfort of the troubled	pray for us
Help of Christians	pray for us
Queen of angels	pray for us
Queen of patriarchs and prophets	pray for us
Queen of apostles and martyrs	pray for us
Queen of confessors and virgins	pray for us
Queen of all saints	pray for us
Queen conceived in grace	pray for us
Queen raised up to glory	pray for us
Queen of the rosary	pray for us
Queen of peace	pray for us
Lamb of God, you take away the sins of the world	have mercy on us
Lamb of God, you take away the sins of the world	have mercy on us
Lamb of God, you take away the sins of the world	have mercy on us

V. Pray for us, holy Mother of God.

R. That we may become worthy of the promises of Christ.

Let us pray.

Eternal God,
let your people enjoy constant health in mind and body.
Through the intercession of the Virgin Mary
free us from the sorrows of this life
and lead us to happiness in the life to come.
Grant this through Christ our Lord.

R. Amen.

— A Marian litany containing some of these invocations was in use in the twelfth century. It was recorded in its present form (apart from a few additions by recent Popes) at Loreto in 1558 and approved by Sixtus V (1521–1590). For about half of the invocations, the present translation uses the traditional renderings which have been in use since the seventeenth century.

23 LITANY OF SAINT JOSEPH

Lord, have mercy	Lord, have mercy
Christ, have mercy	Christ, have mercy
Lord, have mercy	Lord, have mercy
God our Father in heaven	have mercy on us
God the Son, Redeemer of the world	have mercy on us
God the Holy Spirit	have mercy on us
Holy Trinity, one God	have mercy on us
Holy Mary	pray for us
Saint Joseph	pray for us
Noble son of the House of David	pray for us
Light of patriarchs	pray for us
Husband of the Mother of God	pray for us
Guardian of the Virgin	pray for us
Foster father of the Son of God	pray for us
Faithful guardian of Christ	pray for us
Head of the holy family	pray for us
Joseph, chaste and just	pray for us
Joseph, prudent and brave	pray for us
Joseph, obedient and loyal	pray for us
Pattern of patience	pray for us
Lover of poverty	pray for us
Model of workers	pray for us
Example to parents	pray for us
Guardian of virgins	pray for us
Pillar of family life	pray for us
Comfort of the troubled	pray for us
Hope of the sick	pray for us
Patron of the dying	pray for us
Terror of evil spirits	pray for us
Protector of the Church	pray for us

Lamb of God, you take away
  the sins of the world   have mercy on us
Lamb of God, you take away
  the sins of the world   have mercy on us
Lamb of God, you take away
  the sins of the world   have mercy on us

V. God made him master of his household.
R. And put him in charge of all that he owned.

Let us pray.

Almighty God,
in your infinite wisdom and love
you chose Joseph to be the husband of Mary,
the mother of your Son.
As we enjoy his protection on earth
may we have the help of his prayers in heaven.
We ask this through Christ our Lord.

R. Amen.

— Approved by Pius X (1835–1914).

IV
OUR LADY

24 SALVE, REGINA

Hail, holy Queen, Mother of mercy,
hail, our life, our sweetness, and our hope.
To you we cry, the children of Eve;
to you we send up our sighs,
mourning and weeping in this land of exile.
Turn, then, most gracious advocate,
your eyes of mercy toward us;
lead us home at last
and show us the blessed fruit of your womb, Jesus:
O clement, O loving, O sweet Virgin Mary.

> *— One of the four Marian antiphons sung at the end of Night Prayer*
> *according to the season. Possibly by Hermann the Lame, a monk of*
> *Reichenau (1013–1054), or by Adhémar, bishop of Le Puy (d. 1098).*
> *It was used as a processional at Cluny by about 1135.*

25 MEMORARE

Remember, most loving Virgin Mary,
never was it heard
that anyone who turned to you for help
was left unaided.

Inspired by this confidence,
though burdened by my sins,
I run to your protection
for you are my mother.

Mother of the Word of God,
do not despise my words of pleading
but be merciful and hear my prayer.
Amen.

> *— A sixteenth-century abridgement of a fifteenth-century prayer beginning*
> Ad sanctitatis tuae pedes, dulcissima Virgo Maria. *The idea that it was*
> *written by St. Bernard seems to have come from its popularization by*
> *Père Claude Bernard (1588–1641).*

26 ANCIENT PRAYER TO THE VIRGIN

We turn to you for protection,
holy Mother of God.
Listen to our prayers
and help us in our needs.
Save us from every danger,
glorious and blessed Virgin.

> — *This prayer, first found in a Greek papyrus, c. 300,*
> *is the oldest known prayer to the Virgin.*

27 MARY, HELP OF THOSE IN NEED

Holy Mary,
help those in need,
give strength to the weak,
comfort the sorrowful,
pray for God's people,
assist the clergy,
intercede for religious.

May all who seek your help
experience your unfailing protection.
Amen.

> — *Formerly the Magnificat antiphon from the Common*
> *of the Blessed Virgin Mary, Evening Prayer.*

28 A CHILD'S PRAYER TO MARY

Mary, mother whom we bless,
full of grace and tenderness,
defend me from the devil's power
and greet me in my dying hour.

> — *This prayer is from the hymn* Memento rerum conditor. *In some texts it is*
> *added as a last verse to the sixth-century hymn* Quem terra pontus aethera.

29 THE ANGELUS

V. The angel spoke God's message to Mary,
R. and she conceived of the Holy Spirit.

Hail, Mary.

V. "I am the lowly servant of the Lord:
R. let it be done to me according to your word."

Hail, Mary.

V. And the Word became flesh
R. and lived among us.

Hail, Mary.

V. Pray for us, holy Mother of God,
R. that we may become worthy of the promises of Christ.

Let us pray.

Lord,
fill our hearts with your grace:
once, through the message of an angel
you revealed to us the incarnation of your Son;
now, through his suffering and death
lead us to the glory of his resurrection.
We ask this through Christ our Lord.

R. Amen.

> — *The custom of saying the "Hail, Mary" three times when the bell rang in the evening goes back to the thirteenth century, and there are bells of that period inscribed with the angelic salutation. The prayer was formerly the postcommunion for Masses of our Lady in Advent and is now the opening prayer for the Fourth Sunday of Advent.*

30 REGINA CAELI

Queen of heaven, rejoice, alleluia.
  For Christ, your Son and Son of God,
  has risen as he said, alleluia.
  Pray to God for us, alleluia.

V. Rejoice and be glad, O Virgin Mary, alleluia.
R. For the Lord has truly risen, alleluia.

Let us pray.

God of life,
you have given joy to the world
by the resurrection of your Son, our Lord Jesus Christ.
Through the prayers of his mother, the Virgin Mary,
bring us to the happiness of eternal life.
We ask this through Christ our Lord.

R. Amen.

> *— A twelfth-century Evening Prayer antiphon for the Easter Season. Since the thirteenth century, it has been used as the seasonal antiphon in honor of the Blessed Virgin after Night Prayer. From 1743 it has replaced the Angelus in the Easter Season.*

31 A PRIEST'S PRAYER TO MARY

Mother of mercy and love,
blessed Virgin Mary,
I am a poor and unworthy sinner,
and I turn to you in confidence and love.
You stood by your Son
as he hung dying on the cross.
Stand also by me, a poor sinner,
and by all the priests
who are offering Mass today
here and throughout the world.
Help us to offer a perfect and acceptable sacrifice
in the sight of the holy and undivided Trinity,
our most high God.
Amen.

32 PRAYER TO THE VIRGIN MARY

Thanksgiving after Mass

Mary, holy virgin mother,
I have received your Son, Jesus Christ.
With love you became his mother,
gave birth to him, nursed him,
and helped him grow to manhood.
With love I return him to you,
to hold once more,
to love with all your heart,
and to offer to the Holy Trinity
as our supreme act of worship
for your honor and for the good
of all your children.

Mother, ask God to forgive my sins
and to help me serve him more faithfully.
Keep me true to Christ until death,
and let me come to praise him with you
for ever and ever.
Amen.

V
ANGELS AND
SAINTS

33 PRAYER TO SAINT JOSEPH

Blessed Joseph, husband of Mary, be with us this day.

You protected and cherished the Virgin;
loving the Child Jesus as your Son,
you rescued him from danger of death.
Defend the Church, the household of God,
purchased by the blood of Christ.

Guardian of the holy family,
be with us in our trials.
May your prayers obtain for us
the strength to flee from error
and wrestle with the powers of corruption
so that in life we may grow in holiness
and in death rejoice in the crown of victory.
Amen.

*— Leo XIII (1810–1903) encouraged the recitation of this prayer
after the Rosary and the Litany of Loreto during October.*

34 PRAYER TO THE GUARDIAN ANGEL

Angel sent by God to guide me,
be my light and walk beside me;
be my guardian and protect me;
on the paths of life direct me.

———

35 INVOCATION TO SAINTS PETER AND PAUL

Saints Peter and Paul, pray for us.

Lord, come to the aid of your people,
who rely on the help of your holy apostles;
protect us and be our defense for ever.
We ask this through Christ our Lord.
Amen.

> — *This prayer is the postcommunion of the votive Mass of*
> *Saints Peter and Paul in the Roman Missal of 1570.*

VI
TIMES AND
OCCASIONS

36 PRAYER AT THE BEGINNING OF THE DAY

Almighty God,
you have given us this day:
strengthen us with your power
and keep us from falling into sin,
so that whatever we say or think or do
may be in your service and for the sake of your kingdom.
We ask this through Christ our Lord.
Amen.

> — *This prayer is one of the collects from the office of Prime,*
> *which from the sixth century onwards was said just after dawn.*

37 VENITE, EXSULTEMUS

Come, let us sing to the Lord;
   and shout with joy to the Rock who saves us.
Let us approach him with praise and thanksgiving
   and sing joyful songs to the Lord.

The Lord is God, the mighty God,
   the great king over all the gods.
He holds in his hands the depths of the earth
   and the highest mountains as well.
He made the sea; it belongs to him,
   the dry land, too, for it was formed by his hands.

Come, then, let us bow down and worship,
   bending the knee before the Lord, our maker.
For he is our God and we are his people,
   the flock he shepherds.

Today, listen to the voice of the Lord:
Do not grow stubborn, as your fathers did
   in the wilderness,
when at Meriba and Massah
   they challenged me and provoked me,
Although they had seen all of my works.

Forty years I endured that generation.
I said: "They are a people whose hearts go astray
   and they do not know my ways."
So I swore in my anger,
   "They shall not enter into my rest."

Glory to the Father, and to the Son, and to the Holy Spirit:
   as it was in the beginning, is now, and will be for ever. Amen.

— Psalm 95

38 COME, HOLY SPIRIT

V. Come, Holy Spirit, fill the hearts of your faithful.
R. And kindle in them the fire of your love.

V. Send forth your Spirit and they shall be created.
R. And you will renew the face of the earth.

Let us pray.

Lord,
by the light of the Holy Spirit
you have taught the hearts of your faithful.
In the same Spirit
help us to relish what is right
and always rejoice in your consolation.
We ask this through Christ our Lord.

R. Amen.

> — *The first versicle and response adapted from the alleluia verse before the gospel of Pentecost; the second versicle and response from the third antiphon for the Office of Readings on Pentecost; the prayer from the votive Mass of the Holy Spirit in* The Roman Missal.

39 PRAYER OF THANKSGIVING

We give you thanks
for all your gifts,
almighty God,
living and reigning
now and for ever.
Amen.

> — *This prayer is a traditional form of grace after meals.*

40 PRAYER FOR BENEFACTORS

Reward those who have been good to us
for the sake of your name, O Lord,
and give them eternal life.
Amen.

41 PRAYER FOR ALL OCCASIONS

Lord,
may everything we do
begin with your inspiration
and continue with your help,
so that all our prayers and works
may begin in you
and by you be happily ended.
We ask this through Christ our Lord.
Amen.

> *— Formerly the collect for Ember Saturday in Lent, this prayer is
> now used on the Thursday after Ash Wednesday.*

Lord, I believe in you: increase my faith.
I trust in you: strengthen my trust.
I love you: let me love you more and more.
I am sorry for my sins: deepen my sorrow.

I adore you as my first beginning,
I long for you as my last end,
I praise you as my constant helper
and call on you as my loving protector.

Guide me by your wisdom,
correct me with your justice,
comfort me with your mercy,
protect me with your power.

I offer you, Lord,
my thoughts: to be fixed on you;
my words: to have you for their theme;
my actions: to reflect my love for you;
my sufferings: to be endured for your greater glory.

I want to do what you ask of me:
in the way you ask,
for as long as you ask,
because you ask it.

Lord, enlighten my understanding,
strengthen my will,
purify my heart,
and make me holy.

Help me to repent of my past sins
and to resist temptation in the future.
Help me to rise above my human weaknesses
and to grow stronger as a Christian.

Let me love you, my Lord and my God,
and see myself as I really am:
a pilgrim in this world,
a Christian called to respect and love

all whose lives I touch,
those in authority over me
or those under my authority,
my friends and my enemies.

Help me to conquer anger with gentleness,
greed with generosity,
apathy with fervor.
Help me to forget myself
and reach out toward others.
Make me prudent in planning,
courageous in taking risks.
Make me patient in suffering, unassuming in prosperity.

Keep me, Lord, attentive at prayer,
temperate in food and drink,
diligent in my work,
firm in my good intentions.

Let my conscience be clear,
my conduct without fault,
my speech blameless,
my life well-ordered.

Put me on guard against my human weaknesses.
Let me cherish your love for me,
keep your law,
and come at last to your salvation.

Teach me to realize that this world is passing,
that my true future is the happiness of heaven,
that life on earth is short,
and the life to come eternal.

Help me to prepare for death
with a proper fear of judgment,
but a greater trust in your goodness.
Lead me safely through death
to the endless joy of heaven.

Grant this through Christ our Lord.
Amen.

— Attributed to Pope Clement XI (1649–1721).

43 MISERERE

Have mercy on me, God, in your kindness.
In your compassion blot out my offense.
O wash me more and more from my guilt
and cleanse me from my sin.

My offenses truly I know them;
my sin is always before me.
Against you, you alone, have I sinned;
what is evil in your sight I have done.

That you may be justified when you give sentence
and be without reproach when you judge.
O see, in guilt I was born,
a sinner was I conceived.

Indeed you love truth in the heart;
then in the secret of my heart teach me wisdom.
O purify me, then I shall be clean;
O wash me, I shall be whiter than snow.

Make me hear rejoicing and gladness,
that the bones you have crushed may revive.
From my sins turn away your face
and blot out all my guilt.

A pure heart create for me, O God,
put a steadfast spirit within me.
Do not cast me away from your presence,
nor deprive me of your holy spirit.

Give me again the joy of your help;
with a spirit of fervor sustain me,
that I may teach transgressors your ways
and sinners may return to you.

O rescue me, God, my helper,
and my tongue shall ring out your goodness.
O Lord, open my lips
and my mouth shall declare your praise.

For in sacrifice you take no delight,
burnt offering from me you would refuse,
my sacrifice, a contrite spirit.
A humbled, contrite heart you will not spurn.

In your goodness, show favor to Zion:
rebuild the walls of Jerusalem.
Then you will be pleased with lawful sacrifice,
holocausts offered on your altar.

Glory to the Father, and to the Son, and to the Holy Spirit:
    as it was in the beginning, is now, and will be for ever. Amen.

— Psalm 51.

44 ACT OF FAITH, HOPE, AND LOVE

My God, I believe in you,
I trust in you,
I love you above all things,
with all my heart and mind and strength.
I love you because you are supremely good and worth loving;
and because I love you,
I am sorry with all my heart for offending you.
Lord, have mercy on me, a sinner.
Amen.

45 ACT OF CONTRITION

My God,
I am sorry for my sins with all my heart.
In choosing to do wrong
and failing to do good,
I have sinned against you
whom I should love above all things.
I firmly intend, with your help,
to do penance,
to sin no more,
and to avoid whatever leads me to sin.

Our Savior Jesus Christ
suffered and died for us.
In his name, my God, have mercy.

— This prayer is taken from the revised Rite of Penance, *1974.*

46 PRAYER FOR THE POPE

Let us pray for *N.*, our pope.

May the Lord protect him
and grant him length of days.
Amen.

May the Lord be his shield
and deliver him from all harm.
Amen.

May the Lord give him happiness and peace
all the days of his life.
Amen.

> — *This versicle and its response were formerly sung
> at the end of the litany of the saints.*

47 PRAYER FOR UNITY

Almighty and eternal God,
you gather the scattered sheep
and watch over those you have gathered.

Look kindly on all who follow Jesus, your Son.

You have marked them with the seal of one baptism,
now make them one in the fullness of faith
and unite them in the bond of love.
We ask this through Christ our Lord.
Amen.

> — *This prayer is an adaptation of the opening prayer
> from the votive Mass for Christian Unity.*

48 PRAYER FOR MEETINGS

We stand before you, Holy Spirit,
conscious of our sinfulness,
but aware that we gather in your name.

Come to us, remain with us,
and enlighten our hearts.

Give us light and strength
to know your will,
to make it our own,
and to live it in our lives.

Guide us by your wisdom,
support us by your power,
for you are God,
sharing the glory of Father and Son.

You desire justice for all:
enable us to uphold the rights of others;
do not allow us to be misled by ignorance
or corrupted by fear or favor.

Unite us to yourself in the bond of love
and keep us faithful to all that is true.

As we gather in your name
may we temper justice with love,
so that all our decisions
may be pleasing to you,
and earn the reward
promised to good and faithful servants.
Amen.

> — *This prayer, used before each meeting of commissions of the
> Second Vatican Council, is attributed to St. Isidore of Seville (c. 560–636)
> and is included in the prayers for the opening of a synod in the
> Roman Pontifical (1596).*

49 PRAYER FOR THE DEAD

Eternal rest grant to them, O Lord,
and let perpetual light shine upon them.

*— This is the traditional Introit from the Mass for the Dead,
the Requiem Aeternam.*

---

50 DE PROFUNDIS

Out of the depths I cry to you, O Lord,
Lord, hear my voice!
O let your ears be attentive
to the voice of my pleading.

If you, O Lord, should mark our guilt,
Lord, who would survive?
But with you is found forgiveness:
for this we revere you.

My soul is waiting for the Lord,
I count on his word.
My soul is longing for the Lord
more than watchman for daybreak.
(Let the watchman count on daybreak
and Israel on the Lord.)

Because with the Lord there is mercy,
and fullness of redemption,
Israel indeed he will redeem
from all its iniquity.

Glory to the Father, and to the Son, and to the Holy Spirit:
as it was in the beginning, is now, and will be for ever. Amen.

— Psalm 130.

51 A Night Prayer

Visit this house,
we beg you, Lord,
and banish from it
the deadly power of the evil one.
May your holy angels dwell here
to keep us in peace,
and may your blessing be always upon us.
We ask this through Christ our Lord.
Amen.

> *— The traditional closing prayer of Night Prayer,*
> *now used at Night Prayer on Sunday.*

52 Prayer for the Household

Hear us, Lord,
and send your angel from heaven
to visit and protect,
to comfort and defend
all who live in this house.
Amen.

> *— This prayer was formerly used as the conclusion to the*
> *Rite of Sprinkling at the principal Mass on Sundays.*

VII
INVOCATIONS

53 INVOCATIONS

Father.

Jesus.

Praised be Jesus Christ.

Lord, I believe in you.

Lord, I adore you.

Lord, I hope in you.

Lord, I love you.

All for love of you.

Thanks be to God.

Let us bless the Lord.

Your kingdom come.

Your will be done.

As God wills.

Help me, O God.

Strengthen me, Lord.

Lord, hear me.

Lord, save me.

Lord, have mercy.

Lord, spare me.

Lord, do not abandon me.

Glory to God in the highest.

Lord, how great you are.

Praise the Lord!

Alleluia!

Amen.

Come, Lord Jesus!

Hail, Mary.

We adore you, O Christ, and we bless you:
because by your holy cross you have redeemed the world.

Blessed be the Holy Trinity.

Christ is victor, Christ is ruler, Christ is Lord of all.

Heart of Jesus, burning with love for us,
inflame our hearts with love for you.

Heart of Jesus, I trust in you.

Heart of Jesus, all for love of you.

Sacred Heart of Jesus, have mercy on us.

My God and my all.

Lord, be merciful to me, a sinner.   Luke 18:13

Let me praise you, Virgin most holy:
give me strength against your enemies.

Teach me to do your will, for you are my God.   Psalm 143:10

Lord, increase our faith.   Luke 17:5

Lord, I believe; help my unbelief.   Mark 9:24

Lord, make our minds one in truth
and our hearts one in love.

Lord, save us or we perish.   Matthew 8:25

My Lord and my God.   John 20:28

Loving heart of Mary, be my refuge.

Glory to the Father, and to the Son, and to the Holy Spirit:
as it was in the beginning, is now, and will be for ever. Amen.

Jesus, Mary, and Joseph.

Jesus, Mary, and Joseph, I give you my heart and my soul.
Jesus, Mary, and Joseph, assist me in the hour of my death.
Jesus, Mary, and Joseph, may I die and rest in peace with you.

Jesus, gentle and humble of heart, make my heart like yours.

Matthew 11:29

May the blessed sacrament be praised and adored for ever.

Stay with us, Lord.   Luke 24:29

Mother of sorrows, pray for us.

My Mother, my hope.

Lord send laborers into your harvest.   Matthew 9:38; Luke 10:2

All holy men and women, pray for us.

Pray for us, holy Mother of God,
that we may become worthy of the promises of Christ.

Father, into your hands I commend my spirit.   Luke 23:46; Psalm 31:6

Lord Jesus, in your mercy grant them eternal rest.

Queen conceived without original sin, pray for us.

Holy Mother of God, ever Virgin Mary, intercede for us.

Holy Mary, pray for us.

You are the Christ, the Son of the living God.   Matthew 16:26

God is light: in him there is no darkness.   1 John 1:5

God is love: anyone who abides in love, abides in God. 1 John 4:16